CRIME AND DETECTION

C0-BET-764

CAPITAL PUNISHMENT

- Capital Punishment
- Criminal Terminology
- Cyber Crime
- Daily Prison Life
- Domestic Crime
- Famous Trials
- Forensic Science
- Global Terrorism
- Government Intelligence Agencies
- Hate Crimes
- The History of Punishment
- The History of Torture
- Infamous Prisons
- Organized Crime
- Protecting Yourself Against Criminals
- Race and Crime
- Serial Murders
- Unsolved Crimes
- The U.S. Justice System
- The War on Drugs

CRIME AND DETECTION

CAPITAL
PUNISHMENT

Michael Kerrigan

Foreword by Manny Gomez, Esq.

Dorr Township Library
1804 Sunset Dr.
Dorr, MI 49323

LIBRARY OF
CONGRESS
SURPLUS
DUPLICATE

MASON CREST

Mason Crest
450 Parkway Drive, Suite D
Broomall, PA 19008
www.masoncrest.com

Copyright © 2017 by Mason Crest, an imprint of National Highlights, Inc. All rights reserved. No part of this publication may be reproduced or transmitted in any form or by any means, electronic or mechanical, including photocopying, recording, taping, or any information storage and retrieval system, without permission in writing from the publisher.

Printed and bound in the United States of America

First printing
9 8 7 6 5 4 3 2 1

Series ISBN: 978-1-4222-3469-3
Hardcover ISBN: 978-1-4222-3473-0
ebook ISBN: 978-1-4222-8400-1

Library of Congress Cataloging-in-Publication Data on file with the Library of Congress

Developed and Produced by Print Matters Productions, Inc. (www.printmattersinc.com)

Developmental Editor: Amy Hackney Blackwell
Cover and Interior Design: Tom Carling, Carling Design Inc.

Note on Statistics: While every effort has been made to provide the most up-to-date government statistics, the Department of Justice and other agencies compile new data at varying intervals, sometimes as much as ten years. Agency publications are often based on data compiled from a period ending a year or two before the publication date.

CONTENTS

KEY ICONS TO LOOK FOR:

Text-Dependent Questions: These questions send the reader back to the text for more careful attention to the evidence presented there.

Words to Understand: These words with their easy-to-understand definitions will increase the reader's understanding of the text while building vocabulary skills.

Series Glossary of Key Terms: This back-of-the-book glossary contains terminology used throughout this series. Words found here increase the reader's ability to read and comprehend higher-level books and articles in this field.

Research Projects: Readers are pointed toward areas of further inquiry connected to each chapter. Suggestions are provided for projects that encourage deeper research and analysis.

Sidebars: This boxed material within the main text allows readers to build knowledge, gain insights, explore possibilities, and broaden their perspectives by weaving together additional information to provide realistic and holistic perspectives.

FOREWORD

Experience Counts

Detecting crime and catching lawbreakers is a very human endeavor. Even the best technology has to be guided by human intelligence to be used effectively. If there's one truth from my 30 years in law enforcement and security, it's trust your gut.

When I started on the police force, I learned from older officers and from experience what things to look for, what traits, characteristics, or indicators lead to somebody who is about to commit a crime or in the process of committing one. You learn from experience. The older generation of law enforcement teaches the younger generation, and then, if you're good, you pick up your own little nuances as to what bad guys are doing.

In my early work, I specialized in human intelligence, getting informants to tell me what was happening on the street. Most of the time it was people I arrested that I then "flipped" to inform me where the narcotics were being stored, how they were being delivered, how they were being sold, the patterns, and other crucial details.

A good investigator has to be organized since evidence must be presented in a legally correct way to hold up in court. Evidence from a crime scene has to have a perfect chain of custody. Any mishandling turns the evidence to fruits of a poisonous tree.

At my company, MG Security Services, which provides private security to corporate and individual clients in the New York area, we are always trying to learn and to pass on that learning to our security officers in the field.

Certainly, the field of detection has evolved dramatically in the last 100 years. Recording devices have been around for a long time; it's just that now they've gotten really good. Today, a pen can be a video recording device, whereas in the old days it would have been a large box with two wheels. The equipment was awkward and not too subtle: it would be 80 degrees out, you'd be sweating in a raincoat, and the box would start clicking.

The forensic part of detection is very high-tech these days, especially with DNA coming into play in the last couple of decades. A hundred years ago, fingerprinting revolutionized detective work; the next breakthrough is facial recognition. We have recently discovered that the arrangement of facial features (measured as nodes) is unique to each individual. No two people on the planet have the exact same configuration of nodes. Just as it took decades to build out the database of known fingerprints, facial recognition is a work in progress. We will see increasing collection of facial data when people obtain official identification. There are privacy concerns, but we're working them out. Facial recognition will be a centerpiece of future detection and prevention efforts.

Technology offers law enforcement important tools that we're learning to apply strategically. Algorithms already exist that allow retailers to signal authorities when someone makes a suspicious purchase—known bomb-making ingredients, for example. Cities are loaded with sensors to detect the slightest trace of nuclear, biological, or chemical materials that pose a threat to the public. And equipment nested on streetlights in New York City can triangulate the exact block where a gun was fired.

Now none of this does anything constructive without well-trained professionals ready and able to put the information to use. The tools evolve, but what doesn't evolve is human intelligence.

Law enforcement as a community is much better at fighting street and violent crime than it is addressing the newer challenges of cybercrime and terrorism. Technology helps, but it all goes back to human intelligence. There is no substitute for the cop on the street, knowing what is going on in the neighborhood, knowing who the players are. When the cop has quality informants inside gangs, he or she knows when there's going to be a hit, a drug drop, or an illicit transaction. The human intelligence comes first; then you can introduce the technology, such as hidden cameras or other surveillance.

The twin challenges for domestic law enforcement are gangs and guns. Gangs are a big problem in this country. That's a cultural and social phenomenon that law enforcement has not yet found an effective way to counteract. We need to study that more diligently. If we're successful in getting rid of the gangs, or at least diluting them, we will have come a long way in fighting violent crime. But guns are the main issue. You look at England, a first-world country of highly educated people that strictly regulates guns, and the murder rate is minimal.

When it comes to cybercrime, we're woefully behind. That's simply because we hire people for the long term, and their skills get old. You have a twenty-five-year-old who's white-hot now, but guess what? In five years that skill set is lost. Hackers, on the other hand, are young people who tend to evolve fast. They learn so much more than their older law enforcement counterparts and are able to penetrate systems too easily. The Internet was not built with the security of private users in mind. It is like a house with no door locks, and now we're trying to figure ways to secure the house. It was done kind of backward. Nobody really thought that it was going to be this wide-open door to criminal activity.

We need to change the equation for cybercriminals. Right now the chances are they won't get caught; cybercrime offers criminals huge benefits at very little cost. Law enforcement needs to recruit young people who can match skills with the criminals. We also need to work closely with foreign governments and agencies to better identify, deter, and apprehend cybercriminals. We need to make examples of them.

Improving our cybercrime prevention means a lot more talent, a lot more resources, a lot more hands-on collaboration with countries on the outskirts—Russia, China, even Israel. These are the countries that are constantly trying to penetrate our cyberspace. And even if we are able to identify the person overseas, we still need the cooperation of the overseas government and law enforcement to help us find and apprehend the person. Electrical grids are extremely vulnerable to cyberattacks. Utilities built long before the Internet need engineering retrofits to make them better able to withstand attacks.

As with cybercrime, efforts against terrorism must be coordinated to be effective. Communication is crucial among all levels of law enforcement, from local law enforcement and national agencies sharing information—in both directions—to a similar international flow of information among different countries' governments and national bureaus.

In the U.S., since 9/11, the FBI and local law enforcement now share a lot more information with each other locally and nationally. Internationally, as well, we are sharing more information with Interpol and other intelligence and law enforcement agencies throughout the world to be able to better detect, identify, and prevent criminal activity.

When it comes to terrorism, we also need to ramp up our public relations. Preventing terror attacks takes more than a military response. We need to address this culture of death with our own Internet media campaign and 800 numbers to make it easy for people to reach out to law enforcement and help build the critical human infrastructure. Without people, there are no leads—people on the inside of a criminal enterprise are essential to directing law enforcement resources effectively, telling you when to listen, where to watch, and which accounts to check.

In New York City, the populace is well aware of the "see something, say something" campaign. Still, we need to do more. More people need to speak up. Again, it comes down to trusting your instincts. If someone seems a little off to you, find a law enforcement representative and share your perception. Listen to your gut. Your gut will always tell you: there's something hinky going on here. Human beings have a sixth sense that goes back to our caveman days when animals used to hunt us. So take action, talk to law enforcement when something about a person makes you uneasy or you feel something around you isn't right.

We have to be prepared not just on the prevention side but in terms of responses. Almost every workplace conducts a fire drill at least once a year. We need to do the same with active-shooter drills. Property managers today may even have their own highly trained active-shooter teams, ready to be on site within minutes of any attack.

We will never stop crime, but we can contain the harm it causes. The coordinated efforts of law enforcement, an alert and well-trained citizenry, and the smart use of DNA, facial profiles, and fingerprinting will go a long way toward reducing the number and severity of terror events.

Be it the prevention of street crime or cybercrime, gang violence or terrorism, sharing information is essential. Only then can we put our technology to good use. People are key to detection and prevention. Without the human element, I like to say a camera's going to take a pretty picture of somebody committing a crime.

Law enforcement must strive to attract qualified people with the right instincts, team sensibility, and work ethic. At the end of the day, there's no hunting like the hunting of man. It's a thrill, it's a rush, and that to me is law enforcement in its purest form.

MANNY GOMEZ, Esq.
President of MG Security Services,
Chairman of the National Law Enforcement Association,
former FBI Special Agent,
U.S. Marine, and NYPD Sergeant

CHAPTER 1

THE DEATH SENTENCE

Words to Understand

"Bloody Code": popular expression for the list of offenses punishable by death in Britain. It grew in length through the 18th century.

Capital punishment: death as punishment for a crime; also called the death penalty.

Death penalty: capital punishment, death as punishment for a crime.

Democracy: a community or country in which the people control their government.

Execution: the act of killing a person as punishment for a crime.

Exile: the state or period of forced absence from one's country or home.

Intellectual: a person devoted to study and thought, especially about profound or philosophical issues.

Miscreant: one who behaves criminally or viciously

Satirical: relating to the use of wit, irony, or sarcasm to expose human vices and follies.

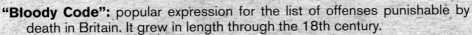

CAPITAL PUNISHMENT IS SURROUNDED WITH SOLEMNITY, FOR NO GRAVER PENALTY COULD BE EXACTED THAN THAT OF DEATH, THE EXTINGUISHING OF AN INDIVIDUAL'S EXISTENCE. NOT THAT IT HAS ALWAYS BEEN THIS WAY. FOR MUCH OF HUMAN HISTORY, A LIFE COULD DEPEND UPON THE WHIM OF A KING, WHILE IN 18TH-CENTURY ENGLAND, A MAN COULD BE HANGED FOR THE THEFT OF A SHEEP.

Reputedly a powerful wizard, and certainly a forceful influence on the feelings of the masses, Lucius Pituanius was viewed with profound suspicion by the authorities in imperial Rome. Finally, in A.D. 30, the Emperor Tiberius declared him an enemy of the state, and he was hurled to his death from the top of the Tarpeian Rock.

Looking at the history of the **death penalty**, and the countless different ways in which it has been used, suggests there is far more to it than simply ending a life. What one civilization sees as a public deterrent, another regards as a private business between the criminal and the law. In some cultures, protracted pain has been part of the punishment; in others, pain has been avoided at all costs. Some societies have used different methods of **execution** for people of different ranks.

There is far more to the story of the death penalty than first meets the eye. Derived from the Latin word *caput*, meaning "head," the term "capital punishment" is used mostly on symbolic grounds, the head being regarded as the seat of life and consciousness in the human body. Today capital punishment as it is exercised in the United States is unmistakably the product of a modern age in terms of both the high-tech methods that are involved and the elaborate legal and psychological safeguards governing its use. At the same time, however, capital punishment has a history that has been many centuries in the making. The purpose of this book is to achieve a better understanding of both.

In Theory

For as long as human civilization has existed, so, too, has the death penalty. Yet some caution has to be exercised in saying this because it is difficult to tell when the tradition of a socially ordered judicial execution separated off from that of human sacrifice aimed at appeasing an irritable deity. Around 1775 B.C., the ruler of Babylon, Hammurabi, laid down the first known system of law. Known as the Code of Hammurabi, it included capital punishment for a number of crimes.

The Fate of Traitors and Murderers in Ancient Rome

In the early days of ancient Rome, traitors were hurled from the Tarpeian Rock, which was located just outside the city. A rough-and-ready sort of justice, it was more elaborate than it sounds. The fall, although high enough to break bones and damage internal organs, was not generally sufficient to kill the person outright. So the victim lay incapacitated at the bottom, unable to move, dying over several days from exposure, hunger, and thirst. Murderers, on the other hand, were tied in sacks and thrown into lakes or rivers to drown.

The Greek philosopher Aristotle turns his back on his beloved Athens, having outraged the authorities by his outspoken opinions: had he remained, he would have found himself facing the death penalty.

There has often been a divide between the attitudes of **intellectuals** to capital punishment and those of society as a whole; this was evident as long ago as classical Athens. The philosopher Aristotle felt that the satisfaction of the one dealing out the punishment or the well-being of the public could not alone justify any punishment. The purpose of any penalty must be the improvement of the offender s character, yet this could hardly be possible if the punishment was death. Aristotle himself would have to leave Athens for a lengthy **exile** under the shadow of the death penalty, having antagonized those in charge of the ancient city.

Athenian statesmen showed little sign of being influenced by arguments against the death penalty. A generation previously in fact, in 399 B.C., the father of all the philosophers, Socrates, had been compelled to commit suicide by drinking hemlock, on the grounds that his teachings "corrupted youth." Athens was the world's first **democracy**, and Socrates, as a free citizen of Athens, had the right

Surrounded by his distraught supporters, Socrates takes the poisonous cup of hemlock that will take his life, establishing a long tradition of suspicion between intellectuals and ruling elites in Western societies.

to commit suicide, which was considered to be a relatively dignified death. Just as he was entitled to vote in elections, the free citizen was allowed to take his own life if found guilty of a crime. Slaves, however, had no such privileges. If found guilty, they were simply beaten to death.

Among the ever practical, down-to-earth Romans, there is little sign of any serious debate. For grave crimes, especially murder, death was the accepted penalty. In the "12 Tables" of the law, the murder of any freeborn Roman was considered equivalent to parricide (the murder of one's father), making it a symbolic offense against authority and the state.

The Romans' concern with reputation and public image is also reflected by the fact that one could be executed for falsely accusing–or even for singing a **satirical** song about–a fellow citizen.

The first Christian martyr, Stephen, is stoned to death by an angry crowd: today, he is revered as a saint. The specter of lynch law, or mob violence, has haunted the entire history of capital punishment, with modern governments going to great lengths to ensure that justice is truly done.

Victims' Justice

Like Christians, Muslims share the scriptures of the Old Testament with Jews, although these texts are seen through the filter of the subsequent teachings of the Prophet Muhammad and other thinkers. The great sacred book of Islam, the Koran, contains the thoughts of God, or Allah, as dictated to the Prophet by an angel, and offers a view of punishment that is similar to biblical tradition. "The free for the free, the slave for the slave, the female for the female," says the famous text, but many scholars insist that this does not mean "a life for a life." The principle, they say, is payment, not punishment; restitution, not revenge. The offender has to do everything in his power to make up for his wrong. So, while allowing the death penalty for various crimes, including murder, shari'a (the formal laws of Islam) has never seen execution as its first preference. For example, the families of murder victims have always been urged to accept financial compensation instead. It is assumed that the decision should rest with them, however, rather than with the court. As the sufferers in the case, it is for their benefit that justice is administered.

The Biblical and the Buddhist

The Hebrew scriptures, on which the whole Western Judeo-Christian tradition is founded, provided a confusing guide to future legislation. Although the Ten Commandments warned "Thou shall not kill," the biblical Old Testament also ordained the death penalty for many civil and religious crimes. This included everything from murder to eating while ritually unclean.

The "new covenant" represented by the Gospels placed far greater emphasis on forgiveness and restraint, although, significantly, some have said, Christ never explicitly calls for the dismantling of the old legal system or the ending of the death penalty. His intervention in the case of the woman taken in adultery (John 8:7), where he says, "He that is without sin among you, let him first cast a stone at her," stops short of suggesting that the victim does not deserve to die. This ambiguity was only underlined by the pronouncement of St. Paul in his Epistle to the Romans (12:19): "Vengeance is mine, I will repay, saith the Lord." Should "Vengeance is mine" be taken to mean "I bring vengeance; I stand for severity of punishment, so you should treat your criminals harshly on my behalf"? Or, on the contrary, did it tell humanity: "Vengeance is mine, not yours, so you should leave punishment to me"? The dispute would continue well into the modern period.

Farther east, in India and beyond, great religions, like Hinduism and Buddhism, find themselves in a similar double bind, committed to the sanctity of life, but aware of the need for society to be governed in peace and order. Many Hindus who refuse to eat meat on ethical grounds still believe that capital punishment has its place in a system of justice.

There are others who strongly disagree with this point of view. The dilemma facing Buddhists is more extreme, since the Buddha whose teachings they follow was more uncompromising in his views. The strict Buddhist would—quite literally—never hurt a fly. The reality seems to be, however, that the more impossibly strict the religious prohibition, the easier it is to ignore. Regimes in Buddhist Myanmar (formerly Burma) and Thailand have shown no qualms about applying the death penalty, although capital punishment in these countries has little to do with religious practice.

In Practice

From the earliest times, the death penalty has been carried out in an enormous variety of ways. The Egyptians are believed to have impaled wrongdoers on wooden stakes and left them to die in the desert sun. This was not only agonizing, but also public, an essential element in many forms of execution to set a warning example to others. This practice was widely used throughout the Middle East, and it grew in sophistication into the method of crucifixion eventually adopted by the Romans. The Gospel accounts of Christ's crucifixion are the best record we have of this terrible punishment. The cause of death was not generally by loss of blood or the trauma of having spikes driven through the feet and hands. Death was usually caused by suffocation due to the crushing pressure on the lungs by the overstretched shoulders and chest muscles.

In medieval Europe, the favored method of capital punishment was hanging. The prisoner dangled from a rope and slowly strangled, a process that could take ten to twenty minutes. Once again, there was an element of public display in the punishment, the victim's body often left hanging long after death.

Hanged, Drawn, and Quartered

For some especially hideous crimes, one death alone was not believed to represent adequate punishment, so authorities began the practice of "hanging, drawing, and quartering." Having been brought close to death by hanging, the victim was taken down, his stomach slit open, and his internal organs "drawn" forth from his abdomen and held up before his horrified eyes. If he survived this terrible ordeal (and a skillful executioner could make sure he did), he would then be "quartered": his body divided into four. Treason, a crime against the king, was seen as a threefold offense, against the king himself, against God, whose representative he was, and against the country. This was the symbolism underlying a punishment that amounted to three executions in one: death by strangulation, death by disembowelment, and death by mutilation.

Off with His Head

Beheading has been a favored form of the death penalty in several civilizations. A quick and comparatively neat method of execution, it was for a long time reserved as a privilege for those well-born individuals who had offended their ruler. This was the case with the English explorer Sir Walter Raleigh, killed on the orders of King James I in 1618. Feeling the edge of his executioner's ax, he is famous for commenting: "This is a sharp medicine, but it is a sure cure for all diseases." He then scornfully rejected the offer of a blindfold, saying, "Think you I fear the shadow of the ax, when I fear not the ax itself?"

The most famous execution of all, shown here in a 15th-century illustration: Jesus Christ is crucified between two thieves. At the foot of the cross, his mother Mary faints from intense grief while, unconcerned, a pair of soldiers play dice over who should have the victims' clothes.

Guy Fawkes and his friends, the Catholic conspirators who had attempted to blow up the English Parliament in the "Gunpowder Plot" of 1605, are dragged through the streets of London on lengths of fencing.

Executed by King James I in 1618 for going beyond his orders as naval commander, Sir Walter Raleigh maintained to the end the self-confident courage that had made him so devastatingly effective—and so dangerously wayward—as a military leader.

Breaking on the Wheel

A particularly brutal method of execution, used as recently as the 18th century in parts of Europe, was known as "breaking on the wheel." This was every bit as crude and cruel as it sounds. The unfortunate prisoner was splayed out across a wheel or X-shaped frame and tied firmly down, and then his limbs were broken in turn with blows from a sledgehammer. He would then be allowed to lie in agony for some hours before the executioner finished him off with a smashing blow to the stomach or chest.

Let This Be a Warning to Others

Anecdotes such as the story of Walter Raleigh hint at an important aspect of capital punishment. Throughout history, it tended to be a type of public performance, with a theater all its own. This trend reached its height in 18th-century England, when under the terms of the notorious **"Bloody Code,"** more than 200 offenses, from shoplifting to sheep stealing, carried the death penalty. Prisoners were paraded through the streets of London to the execution place at Tyburn to warn other **miscreants** what they might expect if they persisted in their criminal ways. So commonplace were these processions, however, that, far from impressing

A thief is publicly beheaded in the China of 1904, his grisly end intended as a warning to those watching. The risk with this sort of ceremony is that, however solemn it may be in theory, it ends up degenerating into a vulgar spectacle that trivializes justice.

the urban poor with their solemnity, they became festive occasions of the most wild and raucous kind, known as the "hanging fair." And rather than setting terrifying examples, the condemned became swaggering heroes. Often, indeed, that state's authority was undermined because the public felt that the punishment was undeserved or, at the very least, too harsh.

The satirical poet Jonathan Swift captured the prevailing mood to perfection:

> *As clever Tom Clinch, while the Rabble was bawling,*
> *Rode stately through Holbourn to die in his calling;*
> *He stopt at the George for a Bottle of Sack,*
> *And promised to pay for it when he'd come back.*

Not everyone saw the amusing side: a less buoyantly satirical writer than Swift, the serious-minded novelist Samuel Richardson was appalled at the behavior of the crowd around the scaffold:

"At the place of execution, the scene grew still more shocking; and the clergyman who attended was more the subject of ridicule than of their serious attention. The psalm was sung amidst the curses and quarrelling of hundreds of the most abandoned and profligate of mankind: upon whom (so stupid are they to any sense of decency) all the preparation of the unhappy wretches seems to serve only for the subject of a barbarous kind of mirth, altogether inconsistent with humanity."

Such drunken carnivals could hardly be said to have any sort of deterrent effect. Thus, through the 19th century, executions were increasingly carried out behind closed doors.

Revolutionary Justice

The guillotine has become the unmistakable symbol of the "Reign of Terror" that followed the French Revolution of 1789, when the king, queen, and thousands of their aristocratic supporters were publicly executed. This does something of an injustice to Ignace Guillotine. He had not invented the machine, but he had perfected it and campaigned for its use for humanitarian reasons. The task of developing a quicker and more painless means of administering capital punishment concerns lawgivers even today, and the contribution Guillotine made was by no means negligible. The idea that the act of beheading might be mechanized was not new. In fact, similar devices had been in use in parts of Europe since medieval times. However, with its triangular blade, the guillotine was by far the quickest, cleanest, and most efficient form of execution.

Text-Dependent Questions

1. Name three old methods of execution.
2. What was the "Bloody Code"?
3. What Latin word meaning "head" gives us the term "capital punishment"? What sort of execution does that term envision?

Research Projects

1. Research medieval execution practices. Are techniques such as breaking on the wheel and burning at the stake considered today to be torture rather than execution?
2. How do major religions such as Christianity, Buddhism, Islam, and Hinduism approach the death penalty? What arguments for and against have been made on religious grounds over the centuries?
3. Why do societies execute people? Pick a historical time and place and find out why and how capital punishment was administered.

CHAPTER 2

AN AMERICAN TRADITION

Words to Understand

Abolition: the act of ending the observance or effect of something, especially relating to laws.

Bifurcated: divided into two branches or parts.

Infallibility: the impossibility of making a mistake.

Mandatory: containing or constituting a command; obligatory.

THE PRINCIPLES OF "LIBERTY, EQUALITY, AND FRATERNITY" SEEM TO HAVE BEEN FORGOTTEN IN THE FRENCH REVOLUTION (1789–1799), WHICH SOON BROKE DOWN INTO A RUTHLESS "REIGN OF TERROR" AND REVENGE, BUT THE IDEALS OF DEMOCRACY WERE STILL BEING DEBATED AND WORKED OUT ACROSS THE ATLANTIC. THERE, THE AMERICAN COLONIES HAD OVERTHROWN ENGLISH RULE AND FOUGHT TO BECOME INDEPENDENT, TO BUILD WHAT ABRAHAM LINCOLN WOULD LATER CALL A "GOVERNMENT OF THE PEOPLE, BY THE PEOPLE, AND FOR THE PEOPLE." ONE OF THE FIRST CHALLENGES FACING THE NEW NATION'S LEADERS AND IMPORTANT THINKERS WAS DECIDING

A portrait of Benjamin Franklin, who believed that, far from discouraging violence, the death penalty effectively promoted it, giving citizens a sense that the life of the individual was held in low regard by their society.

WHETHER, WHEN, AND IN WHAT MANNER THE DEATH PENALTY SHOULD BE APPLIED: HUMANITARIANISM WAS AN IMPORTANT PRINCIPLE. YET SO, TOO, WAS THE NEED FOR JUSTICE, THE IDEA THAT EACH INDIVIDUAL'S FREEDOM SHOULD BE BALANCED WITH THOSE OF HIS OR HER FELLOW CITIZENS, AND THE CENTRAL DEMOCRATIC DUTY OF UPHOLDING THE RULE OF LAW.

The American Debate

Capital punishment is not mentioned in the United States Constitution of 1787. However, this does not mean that it is "unconstitutional." Rather, the framers of the Constitution seem to have taken the use of the death penalty for granted. The Eighth Amendment bars cruel and unusual punishment. It is part of the Bill of Rights (1789), the first 10 amendments, or changes and additions, to the Constitution that protected personal rights and limited the power of government. At that time in history "cruel" punishment meant something other than simple execution. Even so, there were signs of some discomfort with a system substantially inherited from an English one that was associated with the oppression of the American colonies and notorious for the excesses of the "Bloody Code." George Washington's friend and revolutionary inspiration, the French soldier the Marquis de Lafayette, launched his own eloquent plea against its use. He was opposed to the imposition of the death penalty, he said, and expected to remain so until he could be convinced of "the **infallibility** of man." Others, such as Benjamin Rush, Benjamin Franklin, and the the second U.S. Attorney General, William Bradford, opposed the death penalty on the grounds that it had a brutalizing effect on society as a whole. By sending out the message that the state did not seem to value human life, it tended to encourage, rather than minimize, violent crime, they said.

Thomas Jefferson seems to have sympathized, up to a point, at least. As governor of Virginia (1779–1781) and then again as president of the United States (1801–1809), he worked vigorously to reduce the number of crimes for which the death penalty could be applied. Despite this, Jefferson did not want to do away with the death penalty altogether. He may have objected to what he saw as the sheer bloodthirstiness of existing laws; at the same time, he insisted on society's "right to erase from the roll of its members any one who rendered his own existence inconsistent with theirs; to withdraw from him the protection of their laws, and to remove him from among them by exile, or even by death if necessary."

Yet this ultimate measure would only actually be called for, Jefferson was convinced, "for murder and perhaps for treason." Other crimes were best punished "by working on high roads, rivers . . . etc, a certain time proportioned

The French general the Marquis de Lafayette held a simple case against the death penalty. In his belief, it made the possible miscarriage of justice irreversible: what amends could be made to a man or woman who had been incorrectly executed?

Cruel and Unusual?

The Eighth Amendment of the Bill of Rights seems absolutely clear in its prohibition of any "cruel and unusual punishment," until one asks just what would define such a punishment. The fact is that one man's "cruel and unusual punishment" is another's justifiable punishment "to fit the crime." It is ironic that the wording of the American Bill of Rights was taken just about word for word from its English equivalent of 1689, a document that had done nothing to prevent the introduction of the 18th century's "Bloody Code."

to the offense." Under his influence, while capital punishment continued to be used in the United States, it was on nothing like the scale sanctioned by English conventions of the day.

The European View

The French Revolution may have collapsed into carnage, but the mood that first inspired it still lived: a boundless confidence in the capacities, and in the essential goodness, of humankind. Stirred by Englishman Sir Isaac Newton's reordering of the scientific universe, a new generation of progressive thinkers in France, called *philosophes*, had, throughout the 18th century, been celebrating the limitless potential of humankind for progress. At the same time, they were proclaiming the birth of the "Age of Reason," urging their readers to turn their backs on every sort of superstition and barbarity: capital punish-ment, they firmly believed, was both. It also granted the monarch what now seemed an outrageous power over another's life and death. The impact of such thinking was felt throughout the 19th century in just about every corner of the world.

Earlier, in 1764, the Italian philosopher writer Cesare Bonesana Beccaria had written a work entitled *Essay on Crimes and Punishments*, which proved profoundly influential.

> *The punishment of death is pernicious to society, writes Beccaria, "from the example of barbarity it affords. If the passions, or the necessity of war, have taught men to shed the blood of their fellow creatures, the laws, which are intended to moderate the ferocity of mankind, should not increase it by examples of barbarity, the more horrible as this punishment is usually attended with formal pageantry. Is it not absurd, that the laws, which detest and punish homicide, should, in order to prevent murder, publicly commit murder themselves? What must men think, when they see wise magistrates and grave ministers of justice, with indifference and tranquility, dragging a criminal to death, and whilst a wretch trembles with agony, expecting the fatal stroke, the judge, who has condemned him, with the coldest insensibility, and perhaps with no small gratification from the exertion of his authority, quits his tribunal, to enjoy the comforts and pleasures of life? They will say, 'Ah! Those cruel formalities of justice are a cloak to tyranny, they are a secret language, a solemn veil, intended to conceal the sword by which we are sacrificed to the insatiable idol of despotism. Murder, which they would represent to us a horrible crime, we see practiced by them without repugnance or remorse."*

French officials oversee the guillotining of three rebels in an African colony in 1900. In the 19th century, European powers established versions of their own systems in their colonies: many of these countries maintained these traditions even after independence.

CAPTURE OF JOHN BROWN.

A pivotal moment in the Civil War—and, arguably, in the moral history of modern America—was the capture of John Brown at Harpers Ferry. Brown's dignity in meeting death boosted not only his antislavery cause, but also the concern that such executions were out of place in a civilized society.

An American Hanging

"John Brown was hung today," wrote Thomas J. Jackson from Charles Town, in what is now West Virginia, on December 2, 1859. U.S. forces led by Colonel Robert E. Lee had captured the famous antislavery campaigner and 20 of his followers after Brown had raided the federal arsenal in Harpers Ferry as part of an attempt to lead a slave uprising. Jackson, a witness at the public hanging and later a Confederate general, wrote: "He behaved with unflinching firmness. Brown had his arms tied behind him, and ascended the scaffold with apparent cheerfulness. After reaching the top of the platform, he shook hands with several who were standing around him. The sheriff placed the rope around his neck,

John Brown's body might molder in its grave, but, as the song proclaimed, his truth went marching on, an inspiration to the Union forces in the Civil War. Politically motivated executions often rebound on those who carry them out, making the martyr into a focus for the political passions of a people as a whole.

An Anomaly Addressed

The Gregg Ruling of 1976 dealt with the difficulty highlighted most famously by Benjamin Franklin: that laws that are "too severe" are "seldom executed." The introduction of **"bifurcated trials,"** with two separate hearings (one to establish guilt or innocence, then another to decide upon the sentence), helped to deal with the age-old problem of juries' reluctance to convict when they thought a death penalty might follow.

then threw a white cap over his head and asked him if he wished a signal when all should be ready—to which he replied that it made no difference, provided he was not kept waiting too long.

"In this condition he stood on the trap door, which was supported on one side by hinges, and on the other by rope, for about 10 minutes, when Col. S. told the Sheriff, 'All is ready.' A single blow cut the rope, and Brown fell through about 25 inches, so as to bring his knees on a level with the position occupied by his feet before the rope was cut. With the fall, his arms below the elbow flew up, hands clenched, and his arms gradually fell by spasmodic motions—there was very little motion of his person for several minutes, after which the wind blew his lifeless body to and fro—

"I was much impressed with the thought that before me stood a man, in the full vigor of health, who must in a few minutes be in eternity."

The Controversy Continues

The pressure for **abolition** was always there, in 1845 finding a voice in the American Society for the Abolition of Capital Punishment. In 1892 New York representative Newton Curtis introduced a bill for the complete abolition of capital punishment at a federal level. His bid failed, but it prompted a modest revival in the fortunes of the anti-capital punishment movement. In 1897 Congress passed "An Act to Reduce the Cases in Which the Death Penalty May be Inflicted," which did just that, in particular, making the death sentence a matter of the judge's discretion at trial, rather than **mandatory** in every case.

The History

Pennsylvania was the first state to conduct executions within the walls of its prisons in 1834. With its influential Quaker community, Pennsylvania pioneered penal reform, but other states abolished public executions in the course of the 19th century. In 1846 Michigan did away with the death penalty for all crimes except treason; a few years later, Rhode Island and Wisconsin abolished it altogether. However, more than 100 years after Pennsylvania made executions private, Kentucky was still holding executions in front of large crowds.

The states that maintained the tradition of hanging did try to make it more humane, increasingly using the "long drop." Previously, a prisoner had been "turned off" a ladder, platform, or the back of a cart and left to dangle, "dancing" in the air. Now, the neck was noosed with a longer rope and the body placed over an abruptly opening trapdoor, so that the force of the fall snapped the neck, making death instantaneous.

By 1917, 10 states had abolished the death penalty for all crimes, with the exception of treason, yet it would be wrong to assume that abolitionism was making slow yet steady progress. In fact, as the temperature of the debate heated up through the early decades of the 20th century, public opinion swung violently back and forth, polarized by a series of sensational and highly controversial cases.

On July 7, 1865, George Atzerodt, David Herold, Lewis Powell, and Mary Surratt go to their deaths together at Washington's Old Penitentiary. They had conspired with John Wilkes Booth to assassinate Abraham Lincoln: Booth himself was shot dead in the course of his apprehension.

On the one hand, there were the Chicago "Thrill Killers," Richard Loeb and Nathan Leopold Jr., wealthy white students who, in 1924, kidnapped and killed a 14-year-old boy. They were given what many people felt were wholly inadequate life sentences for a crime apparently committed simply for the excitement of it. On the other hand, there were Nicola Sacco and Bartolomeo Vanzetti, two Italian anarchists/revolutionaries dedicated to the total overthrow of government, who were executed in 1927 for a murder committed in the course of an armed robbery aimed at raising funds for their cause. There seems, in truth, to have been good forensic grounds for finding them guilty, but there was also undoubtedly an atmosphere of hysteria in the media at the time. Some ill-advised remarks of the judge, moreover, left many with the feeling that Sacco and Vanzetti had been tried for their political beliefs and not their actions.

Abolished and Reinstated

The arguments continued through the decades that followed, the abolitionist case gaining the most ground, assisted to some extent by tensions between the federal and state systems. A number of high-profile court cases had important implications for the status of capital punishment in the United States. The Supreme Court's decision in the case of *Trop v. Dulles* (1958) had no direct bearing on the death penalty, yet campaigners seized on the judgment that the Eighth Amendment involved an "evolving standard of decency that marked the progress of a maturing society." This was interpreted as meaning that times changed and so did acceptable standards, leaving the way clear for a challenge to the death penalty.

What had been appropriate to the early 19th century might be deemed "cruel and unusual punishment" now. Whatever might be the case in legal theory, the death penalty did seem to be becoming less acceptable in legal practice, especially if the number of actual executions was anything to go by. While there had been 1,289 executions in the United States in the 1940s, the figure dropped to 715 in the 1950s; it fell away to 195 for the 1960s. A national opinion poll in 1966 showed only 42 percent of Americans supporting capital punishment: the practice seemed to be withering away of its own accord. In 1972, it seemed, the death penalty had finally received its own deathblow with the landmark Supreme Court case of *Furman v. Georgia*. In its judgment, the court effectively suspended the death penalty in those 38 states that still exercised it, ruling that under existing statutes, capital punishment did indeed constitute "cruel and unusual punishment."

The merest hint of a "political" execution makes its victim into a potent symbol of state oppression. Sacco and Vanzetti were guilty of the crime for which they were tried, but their names still became a rallying point for radicals mobilizing support for left-wing causes.

This famous photograph, taken with a concealed camera strapped to the ankle of a *New York Daily News* reporter, shows the execution in 1928 of Ruth Snyder for the murder of her husband.

The Supreme Court's objection to the death penalty as applied in Georgia and elsewhere was that, in allowing individual juries to decide when it should be applied, it opened the way to sentencing that was arbitrary and inconsistent and, therefore, unjust. In 1976, however, the state of Georgia was back before the Supreme Court with a proposal that judges guide juries to their decisions along

Apparently in a grave but philosophical mood, Caryl Chessman sits to be photographed at San Quentin prison, in California, just 48 hours before the time appointed for his execution in the prison's gas chamber in February 1960.

consistent guidelines. This was approved, and the death penalty was reinstated. With its implicit acceptance that there was nothing unconstitutional about capital punishment *in principle*, the "Gregg Ruling" opened the way for other states to rewrite their statutes, too.

It has an almost medieval air of clanky obsolescence today, which makes it hard to recall that, when it was introduced 100 years ago, the electric chair appeared to be the last word in modern punishment: efficient, clean, high-tech, and—above all—humane.

Text-Dependent Questions

1. What part of the U.S. Constitution forbids "cruel and unusual punishment"?
2. What did the U.S. Supreme Court decide in *Furman v. Georgia*?
3. Why did thinkers such as Benjamin Franklin oppose the death penalty?

Research Projects

1. Opinions about the death penalty have varied over time. Look at the history of support for capital punishment in the United States When has it been most popular? When has it been least popular? What reasons can you find to explain these trends?
2. Criminals such as Timothy McVeigh and Dzhokhar Tsarnaev kill large numbers of strangers in cold blood. They both sentenced to death for their crimes. Do you think this is the correct punishment for crimes of great magnitude and callousness? Why or why not?
3. What is cruel and unusual punishment? Research this topic, and see if you think the death penalty—including long stays on death row—qualifies as "cruel and unusual."

THE DEATH PENALTY IN PRACTICE

Words to Understand

Conviction: declaration by a judge or jury that an individual is guilty of a crime.

Exoneration: a finding that a convicted person is not in fact guilty of the crime for which he or she has been convicted.

Humane: showing compassion for other human beings or animals.

Humanitarian: concerned with human welfare.

CAPITAL PUNISHMENT IN THE UNITED STATES IS PERFORMED ONLY UNDER STRICTLY LIMITED CONDITIONS. MOST STATES DO NOT USE IT AT ALL. AS OF 2014, 19 STATES AND THE DISTRICT OF COLUMBIA HAD ABOLISHED THE DEATH PENALTY. VERY FEW CATEGORIES OF CRIME CARRY THE DEATH PENALTY. IN MOST STATES, THE DEATH PENALTY CAN BE ADMINISTERED ONLY FOR PREMEDITATED MURDER; A FEW ALSO ALLOW IT FOR CRIMES SUCH AS TREASON AND AGGRAVATED SEXUAL ASSAULT.

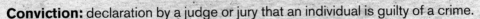
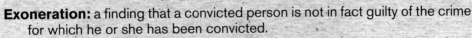

Protesters parade behind a replica electric chair outside the U.S. embassy in Madrid, the Spanish capital.

In 2014 there were only 35 executions in the United States, all of those in just seven states. That year, courts issued the death penalty as a punishment only 72 times. These numbers were part of a dramatic downward trend in enthusiasm for the death penalty in the United States and the world.

For historical reasons, the methods of execution employed vary a good deal from state to state. All states are supposed to take scrupulous care that executed convicts do not suffer physically. The law may call for the giving up of a life, but it emphatically does not allow for physical or mental torture.

While in principle authorities are expected to go to great lengths to ensure that executions do not cause suffering, there is considerable controversy about how effective they have been; evidence that convicts have in fact suffered considerable pain, particularly from sup-

William Mason, a death row prisoner at the Ellis 1 Unit, near Huntsville, Texas, works on the details of an appeal against his **conviction** for murdering his wife. Efforts paid off with a resentencing hearing on the punishment.

posedly **humane** lethal injections, is one of the reasons that many Americans oppose the death penalty. That the state should seem to lean over backward to protect the rights of the man or woman responsible for some especially heinous murder may be a cause of public exasperation, and private anguish for their victims' families. In the end, though, the meticulous observance of even the vilest murderer's rights is our guarantee that we remain a just society.

The Where, Why, and Who

As of 2014, of the 50 American states, 31 had the death penalty, and 19 did not. The states without the death penalty were Alaska, Connecticut, Hawaii, Illinois, Iowa, Maine, Maryland, Massachusetts, Michigan, Minnesota, Nebraska, New Jersey, New Mexico, New York, North Dakota, Rhode Island, Vermont, West Virginia, and Wisconsin. The District of Columbia (Washington, D.C.) abolished the death penalty in 1981.

In this, the United States was following the worldwide trend; as of 2012, over two-thirds of countries had abolished the death penalty or no longer used it. Most executions occurred in just five countries: China, Iran, North Korea, Yemen, and the United States. The United Nations has called several times for a global moratorium on, or legal stop to, executions, and the General Assembly has expressed a desire to see capital punishment eliminated worldwide.

Opponents of the death penalty point to many problems with it. FBI data shows lower homicide rates in states without the death penalty than in states with it, suggesting that the death penalty does not deter crime. A number of death row inmates are mentally ill or mentally disabled. And there is always the worry of executing an innocent person, and lack of confidence in the accuracy of the criminal justice system. Amnesty International noted that between 1973 and 2014, 151 people had been released from death row after new evidence overturned their convictions. In many cases, DNA evidence provides conclusive proof that an individual did not commit a crime. As of 2014, the Innocence Project had helped 330 convicts (not all on death row) earn **exoneration** through DNA evidence examined after their convictions.

More Statistics

According to a 2014 Gallup poll, 63 percent of Americans favored capital punishment for certain murder convictions; a Pew Research Center survey conducted around the same time found that 56 percent of Americans support the death penalty for murderers, and 38 percent are opposed. This is a significant drop from 1996, when 78 percent of people surveyed supported the death penalty. Most of the drop in support occurred among Democrats and women.

The main reason cited in favor of capital punishment was that execution is equal to the crime, although the number of people citing this as a justification dropped from 50 percent in 1991 to 35 percent in 2014. Even supporters of capital punishment tend to doubt that the death penalty discourages crime, and a majority do worry that there is a risk of an innocent person being executed.

Critics of the death penalty argue that it is disproportionately applied to racial minorities, the poor, and those with intellectual disabilities or mental illness. A large number of these are sentenced to death for killing white victims; it is much less common for people to be sentenced to death for the murder of a black victim.

In 2013 the U.S. Census Bureau reported that 77.7 percent of the U.S. population was white, 13.2 percent was black, and 17.1 percent was Latino. Between 1976 and 2015, states executed 783 white individuals, 490 black individuals, 114 Latinos, and 24 of other races. Nearly 76 percent of the murder victims were white. In the case of interracial murders, there were 294 executions for crimes with a black defendant and a white victim, but only 31 executions for crimes involving a white defendant and a black victim. In 2014 the U.S. death row population included nearly equal numbers of black and white defendants.

Main Methods Used by State

Method	Number of executions 1976–2014	Jurisdictions that authorize these methods of execution
Lethal injection	1,236	Alabama, Arizona, Arkansas, California, Colorado, Connecticut, Delaware, Florida, Georgia, Idaho, Indiana, Kansas, Kentucky, Louisiana, Mississippi, Missouri, Montana, Nebraska, Nevada, New Hampshire, New Mexico, North Carolina, Ohio, Oklahoma, Oregon, Pennsylvania, South Carolina, South Dakota, Tennessee, Texas, Utah, Virginia, military, U.S. government (Connecticut, Nebraska, and New Mexico have repealed the death penalty, but the penalty can still apply to inmates already on death row.)
Electrocution	158	Alabama, Arkansas, Florida, Kentucky, Oklahoma, South Carolina, Tennessee, Virginia
Gas chamber	11	Arizona, California, Maryland, Missouri, Wyoming
Hanging	3	Delaware, New Hampshire, Washington
Firing squad	3	Oklahoma, Utah

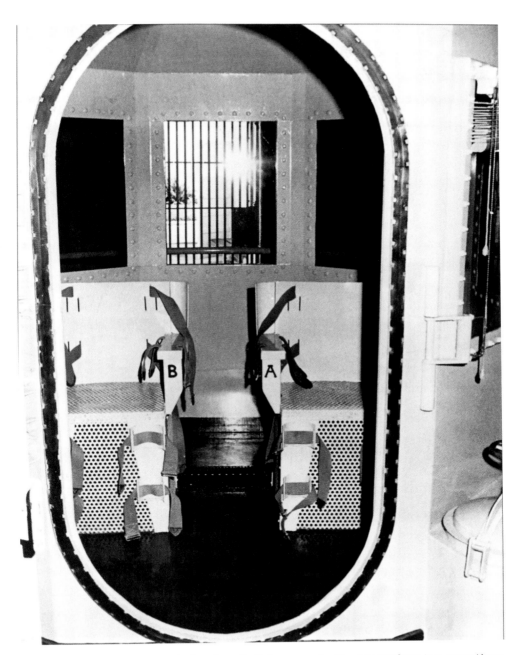

The gas chamber at California's San Quentin Prison was designed to perform two executions at once. Normally, though, executions are conducted individually, with seat B being used in preference, being more accessible to the stethoscope that monitors heartbeats.

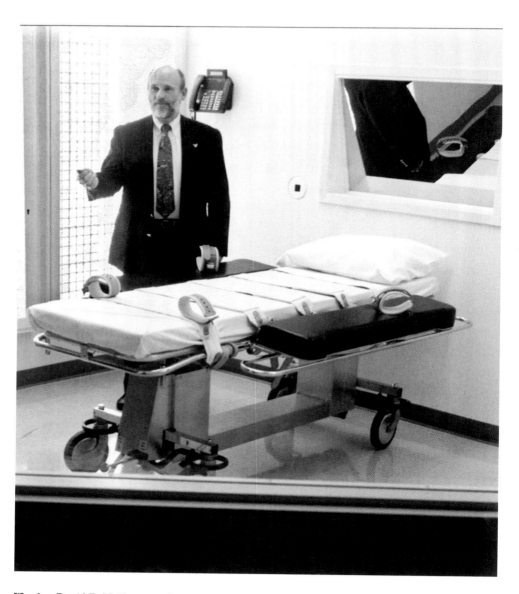

Warden David R. McKune conducts reporters around the execution suite at Kansas' Lansing Correctional Facility.

The Novelist's Song

"You commit a murder Monday and commit a murder Tuesday. I wasn't waiting for Wednesday to come around." So said Brenda Nicol of Provo, Utah, before turning in her cousin Gary Gilmore (pictured), whom she had looked after in her home while he was out on parole from an armed robbery sentence in the summer of 1976. Gilmore had indeed committed two murder-robberies in two days. The Utah court had little alternative but to order his execution. Yet, with the death penalty only just reintroduced in the wake of *Gregg v. Georgia*, there is little doubt that the condemned man could have extended his time on death row with a series of appeals. Gilmore, however, refused to play what he saw as a legalistic game.

The desperate courage of this criminal struck some kind of chord with writer Norman Mailer, although he was impressed as well with the integrity of Brenda Nicol. Begun just after Gilmore's death, Mailer's famous book *The Executioner's Song* (1979) explores many of the complex ethical issues caused by the system as it stands, and the self-destructive victory Gilmore strove so hard to win by his refusal to "play ball."

Tracy Housel's execution in Georgia, in 2002, gave rise to trans-Atlantic tensions on account of his United States-British dual citizenship. The effect on public opinion was muted, though: while Britain did away with the death penalty decades ago, many ordinary people clearly regret its abolition.

Convicted of a brutal murder, 23-year-old Jack Sullivan went to his death with a smile and a cigar, wisecracking even as he was strapped down in his seat in the gas chamber in the Arizona State Prison in Florence, Arizona, on May 15, 1936.

How the Death Penalty Is Administered

Capital punishment has come a long way from the days of the rowdy "hanging fair." Today there is great concern that executions take place in a humane manner that does not cause undue suffering to the person being executed. Different states use different methods of execution, but minimizing suffering is always given high importance. There is also emphasis on preventing trauma to the executioner; few people enjoy taking someone else's life, and correctional employees who are required to carry out executions often suffer from emotional turmoil.

Electric Chair

In the latter part of the 19th century, growing **humanitarian** concern came together with a general climate of technological progress to produce a major push to find a more "modern" method of execution. At a time when the wonders of electricity seemed to be transforming every other area of life, what could be more natural than that it should change capital punishment, too? Genuine humanitarian excitement greeted the first use of the electric chair, in New York in 1890, for the execution of ax murderer William Kemmler. "We live in a higher civilization from this day on," was one witness's report. "The man never suffered a bit of pain," claimed executioner's assistant George Fell. There seems to have been a certain amount of wishful thinking in both remarks. In fact, the electrical current failed to kill Kemmler at the first attempt, so the chair had to be charged up again and the whole process repeated.

The first "modern" method of execution, the electric chair was progressively improved as time went on. Although the precise details vary from state to state, there are typically three executioners.

Each throws a switch, but only one will be operating a "live" circuit. Which switch is the live one will not be known to the team, so no one member will have to feel solely responsible afterward. Considerable emotional turmoil may be involved for the person charged by authorities with the taking of another's life, and measures like this minimize that trauma. (This is also why, in those states where execution by firing squad is used, one marksman will traditionally have a blank round in his magazine, so that no marksman will know for certain that he has been responsible for the prisoner's death.)

The electric chair has gradually gone out of favor, after numerous botched executions. A number of executions set defendants on fire and failed to kill them even after multiple shocks. By 2015 only eight states still allowed the use of electric chairs, and all of them used lethal injection as their primary

The heavy, airtight door of today's Arizona gas chamber is a more reliable and humane means of execution than it was in Jack Sullivan's day. Even so, it has gradually been replaced by lethal injection in the majority of cases.

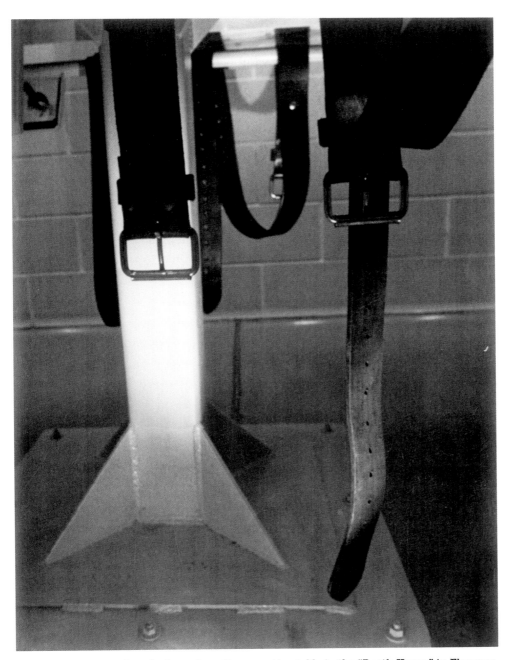

Buckled straps hang loosely down from the execution table in the "Death House" in Florence, Arizona: the straps hold a prisoner down while the lethal injection is administered.

method of execution. Georgia and Nebraska have both ruled that the use of the electric chair is cruel and unusual punishment and not allowed by their state constitutions.

Gas Chambers

The first attempts to use cyanide gas as a means of execution in 1924 also met with practical difficulties. Attempts by prison authorities in Nevada to introduce it to the cell of murderer Gee Jon while he was sleeping proved unsuccessful, so an airtight gas chamber had to be constructed.

The standard gas chamber is made of glass and steel, with an open pan beneath the prisoner's chair. Once the prisoner has been strapped in and the chamber sealed, hydrochloric acid is piped into the pan, after which potassium cyanide or sodium cyanide is dropped into the acid by mechanical means. The two compounds react to produce highly poisonous hydrocyanic gas, which causes unconsciousness in seconds, and death itself in a matter of minutes. As with other methods, a number of executioners may be involved and "dummy" equipment used, so that nobody knows for sure which one of them has actually brought about the prisoner's death.

In 2014 only 11 states still used the gas chamber, and all of those used lethal injection as a primary method.

Lethal Injection

In the late 20th century, lethal injection became the most widespread form of execution in the United States. In this method, a doctor hooks the condemned prisoner up to an intravenous drip and administers various drugs.

Lethal injection was intended to be a perfect, humane method of execution, but in practice it has turned out not to be foolproof. If the prisoner has had a history of heavy intravenous drug use, it can be hard to find a suitable vein. Some executions have been botched by poor technique, and the prisoners have been in obvious pain. In 2014 the execution of Joseph Wood in Arizona required 15 injections of drugs and still took over two hours, during which he gasped and gulped. That same year Oklahoma's execution of Clayton Lockett took over 45 minutes of writhing and gasping.

Part of the problem is that there is no consistent drug protocol for lethal injection, so states have been experimenting. During the first years of lethal injection, many states used a three-drug sequence: the anesthetic sodium thiopental, a paralyzing drug called pancuronium bromide, and potassium chloride

Death penalty protesters rally outside the Maryland state house in support of the governor's efforts to repeal the state's death penalty.

to stop the heart and cause death. This method has largely disappeared because the necessary drugs are unavailable; European drug companies refuse to sell drugs to be used in executions. Some states use a single dose of an anesthetic. Some states used single doses of the anesthetic pentobarbital in the 2010s, but by 2015 several had run out of the drug and could not buy more from the Danish manufacturer.

States that wanted to continue executing prisoners had to come up with alternate methods to replace lethal injection. In 2015 Nebraska enacted a law allowing the use of nitrogen gas for executions if lethal injection drugs were unavailable. Utah's governor signed a law authorizing the use of firing squads instead. Georgia postponed all executions that year until the drugs used for executions could be analyzed to ensure that they were effective.

Even in those states most apparently committed to the use of the death penalty, strong "anti" organizations have emerged: here, protesters march in force outside the state capitol building in Austin, Texas. Texas has one of the most active death penalty policies in the United States.

Text-Dependent Questions

1. What methods are used for executions in the United States?
2. What are some of the drawbacks of the electric chair?
3. Why is lethal injection currently the primary method of execution used in the United States?
4. Why are some states finding it difficult to carry out lethal injections?

Research Projects

1. In states that have abolished the death penalty, what was the process of event and argument that led to this decision? In states that retain the death penalty, what are the main reasons?
2. Research lethal injection. Why was it introduced? How is it supposed to work? What criticisms have been made of it?
3. Choose a well-known convict who has been executed. Find contemporary news stories describing his experience on death row and the process of the execution. Did the execution go smoothly? What were the reactions to the event?

CHAPTER 4

THE DEATH PENALTY WORLDWIDE

Words to Understand

Communism: political and economic system in which the major productive resources, such as factories, mines, and farms, are owned by the public or the state.

Hypocrisy: pretending to be what one is not or to believe what one does not

Penal: relating to penalties or prisons.

Reprieve or stay of execution: calling of a temporary halt to an execution to allow all legal challenges to be explored.

Scapegoat: someone who is unfairly blamed for something others have done.

THE UNITED STATES IS ONE OF COMPARATIVELY FEW COUNTRIES THAT NOW HAS THE DEATH PENALTY, A SITUATION THAT HAS EXPOSED IT TO SOME CRITICISM.

The guillotine has become the most immediately recognizable symbol of the French Revolution, and the painting shows a typical execution scene during the period infamously known as the "Reign of Terror," when members of the French aristocracy were beheaded one after another: few now realize that the guillotine was originally introduced as a humanitarian reform.

The *Furman v. Georgia* Supreme Court decision of 1972 halted capital punishment for a time in the United States. This move simply seemed to bring the United States into line with most Western countries. Two centuries of reform had seen capital punishment disappearing by degrees from all the major countries of the developed world.

In taking steps to reintroduce the death penalty four years later, the United States was turning its back on the crowd, favoring its own independent conscience over international standards. Since that time, public support for capital punishment has gone up and down. Executions rose steadily until they peaked around 2000, but since that time they have dropped again. International disapproval has played a part in this drop; in a practical sense, it has become harder to perform lethal injections because European drug manufacturers refuse to supply the necessary drugs. Americans continue to support the death penalty, especially for heinous and public crimes such as the 2013 Boston Marathon bombing, for which Dzhokhar Tsarnaev was sentenced to death in 2015.

But at the same time, there was growing concern on both sides of the political spectrum that the death penalty is not a good solution to the problems it is meant to address. The crime rate plummeted during the 2000s, making the punishment seem less necessary. States have prisons where violent criminals can be safely secured for years. Death row is expensive; convicts often spend years there awaiting execution, during which time taxpayers must pay for their upkeep and multiple appeals. Executing a criminal costs six to eight times what it costs to imprison someone for life.

Former Massachusetts high school wrestler and ethnic Chechen Dzhokhar Tsarnaev received the death penalty for bombing the Boston Marathon in 2013.

The U.S. Supreme Court has considered various death penalty cases over the years. In 2015 they heard a case from three death row inmates who wanted to bar the use of the drug midazolam in lethal injections, claiming that it caused excruciating pain. The Court decided not to ban the drug, arguing that they were not convinced that the drug did cause pain or that there was a better option. But four of the nine justices dissented, and two of them actually questioned whether the death penalty was even permitted by the Constitution, which bars "cruel and unusual punishment."

Dying Out?

That same spirit of the Enlightenment that had done so much to form the thinking of Americans such as Benjamin Franklin and Thomas Jefferson influenced leaders in many other parts of the world as well. Ironically, its effects had been felt first of all, not where popular movements had agitated for it, but where strong monarchs had imposed it of their own free will. In what had then long been regarded as the most backward country in Europe—Russia—the Empress Elizabeth abolished the death penalty by royal decree in 1744. Prussian strongman Frederick the Great (1712–1786) followed suit a few years later. Joseph II of Austria (1741–1790) concluded the reforms of his late mother, the Empress Maria Theresa (1717–1780), by ending capital punishment throughout what had once been the Holy Roman Empire. By the beginning of the 20th century, the death penalty had fallen into disuse across much of Europe (although it would not actually be abolished in Italy until 1994).

Today, no more than a small, central-European nation, Austria was once the heart of a mighty empire: Joseph II's renunciation of the death penalty had an impact across 18th-century Europe and beyond.

Five revolutionaries are put to death in St. Petersburg in 1881, the presence of the priests not disguising the cruelty of the proceedings. The last decades of czarist rule saw Russia spiral into judicial savagery, as terrorist outrages met with vicious reprisals from the authorities.

Simón Bolívar and the other great 19th-century liberators of Latin America also looked to the ideas of the Enlightenment as the inspiration in their nationalist programs. The republics they created represented these values, in however flawed a form. Countries like Venezuela and Ecuador, for instance, were leaders in abolishing the death penalty.

There were, however, backward steps as well. Struggling against revolutionaries, the late czars of Russia had little time for maintaining Elizabeth's high-minded reforms. And there were also, inevitably, **hypocrisies**. When the **Communist** Bolsheviks succeeded in supplanting the czars in 1917, one of their first acts was the abolition of capital punishment. Execution was, however, to be a predominant theme of the next few decades, when the Soviet state killed criminals, actual and political, by the thousands.

The Bloody Code

Britain, home of the "Bloody Code," and as skeptical about Enlightenment ideas as about other things French, had long held out against the abolitionist tide that had been sweeping Europe. Even so, the number of crimes punishable by death dropped significantly in the course of the 19th century, while through the 20th century, the number of executions continued to fall.

As in the United States, all it took was for a single sensational case to make an enormous difference to how people felt. The case of Craig and Bentley in 1952, for example, caused great concern. Chris Craig, age 16, and Derek Bentley, age 19, broke into a South London warehouse. When cornered on the roof by police officers, Craig produced a gun and fired, apparently killing Constable Sydney Miles. There was no suggestion that the mentally backward Bentley had fired the fatal shot, or even been armed, and he had already been arrested when the offense took place. However, Craig was too young to hang, and Bentley had been his willing partner in a "joint venture." Accordingly, he was convicted of murder and executed.

Evidence would emerge much later to suggest that the "murdered" officer had fallen to "friendly fire" from police marksmen, and Bentley's "confession" looked highly dubious, his interrogators having forged his semiliterate signature six times. Yet many people felt from the first that the wretched Bentley had been made a scapegoat and had died the victim of a cruel and vindictive legal system.

A Tale of Two Women

Ruth Ellis has her place in penal history as the last woman to have been hanged in Britain, in 1955. The manager of a London nightclub, she had murdered her lover, David Blakely. Hers was undoubtedly a sad story: Blakely had been faithless, and on occasion, violent. He had cruelly stirred up Ellis's jealousy and laughed at her anguish. Yet she herself did not dispute that she had shot him dead or that she had come armed to seek him out and shoot him. Indeed, she had borrowed the revolver from a friend for this specific purpose. However, her death sentence threw Britain's press and public into turmoil. Thousands signed petitions for her reprieve (although there were no grounds), and her execution lent enormous impetus to the campaign for the abolition of capital punishment.

"Debtors' Door," as it was commonly known, in London's Newgate Prison, was, for many hundreds of prisoners, an exit from life: it was through here that the condemned man or woman was led to the scaffold.

Guilty though she plainly was, Ruth Ellis was seen as a martyr by the British public: her execution helped advance the cause of abolition in that country.

That was duly passed by Parliament a decade later, but barely was the ink on the statute dry than the country was shocked by news from northern England of the "Moors Murders." A young couple, Ian Brady and Myra Hindley, were found to have abducted and murdered a number of children on the moors (wild wasteland) in the hills above Manchester. The victims had been raped and tortured before they were killed, it seemed. In at least one case, their murderers had taped the proceedings.

Brady had clearly been the dominant partner, but there could be no doubt whatsoever of Hindley's close support. In particular, it was she who approached the children to gain their confidence prior to their kidnappings. With her brassy bleached-blond hairdo, she was reminiscent of Ruth Ellis in looks, but Myra Hindley was destined to evoke a very different public reaction. For four decades, she has arguably been Britain's best-known icon of evil, and people's nostalgia for the days of the death penalty can be said to have begun with her. What makes people particularly uncomfortable is the possibility that someone guilty of such a crime should ever be released.

An Execution in China

Pro-democracy campaigner Harry Wu has described the day in 1983 when he stepped out into the streets of Zhengzhou, Henan Province, to find the place deserted. "In a city of two million," he recalled, "it seemed that all work and school had come to a stop. I estimated later that close to half the city's population must have left their jobs and classrooms." Soon, he came upon the crowd, lining a main route through town, he wrote, then, "45 flatbed trucks, one after another, rolled by...at the front of each truck bed, just behind the cab, stood a condemned man bound with heavy rope. The rope ran in an X across his chest and around to his back, holding in place a tall narrow sign. On the top half of each sign was an accusation: 'Thief,' 'Murderer,' 'Rapist.' On the bottom half was the name of the accused, marked through with a large red X."

The procession threaded its way through the town to wind up at a field in the outskirts. There, the prisoners were forced to kneel beside shallow graves before each was killed with a single shot to the back of the head.

Supporters of the human rights group Amnesty International in Hong Kong have protested outside the territory's Chinese and American missions, voicing their objections to the use of capital punishment by both countries.

After Britain's abolition of the death penalty in 1965, most of the Commonwealth followed suit: the countries of the former British Empire still had close cultural and political ties. In Africa, Angola and Mozambique had abolished capital punishment, along with their Portuguese "mother country," in the middle of the 19th century. Although strained by the ravages of civil war, the reform would at least, in principle, survive the transition to independence.

Capital punishment around the world is not always administered with scrupulous care. Human rights groups claim that these alleged "mutineers" in Guinea, West Africa, are being subjected to what amounts to a crude show trial.

Scotsman Kenny Richey spent 21 years on Ohio's death row before his conviction was overturned.

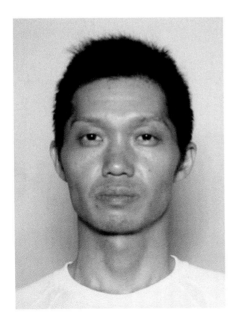

Tsukasa Kanda was hanged on June 25, 2015, in the 12th execution since the December 2012 launch of the Japanese government headed by Prime Minister Shinzo Abe. Kanda was convicted of killing a woman in 2007 in Nagoya, central Japan, after he and his two accomplices met via an Internet site for finding "crime partners."

Kerry Max Cook was exonerated after 22 years on death row, went on to write a popular book about his experience, and is shown here addressing a concert sponsored by Amnesty International.

Text-Dependent Questions

1. Has the United States ever abolished the death penalty?
2. What device was used to execute prisoners during the French Revolution?
3. How did the Enlightenment affect opinions and laws about capital punishment?

Research Projects

1. What was the French Revolution? What role did the guillotine play in it? Why did the guillotine's inventor envision it as an improvement over earlier methods of execution?
2. A number of European nations abolished the death penalty during the 18th and 19th centuries. Why? What philosophical writers influenced their decisions?
3. Investigate the execution practices of nations such as China, Iran, and Afghanistan. How many people are executed there? What methods do they use? Are executions used to stop crimes or as a method of political repression?

Dorr Township Library
1804 Sunset Dr.
Dorr, MI 49323

CHAPTER 5

DEATH ROW

Words to Understand

Death row: the area of a prison where prisoners who have been sentenced to death are incarcerated awaiting execution.

Pardon: decision of a state governor (or, in the case of a "presidential pardon," the president of the United States) to free a prisoner from all legal consequences of a particular offense.

Prosecutor: the lawyer responsible for arguing cases against accused criminals on behalf of the state.

THE PEOPLE WHOSE RESPONSIBILITY IT IS TO ADMINISTER THE DEATH PENALTY IN AMERICA—POLITICIANS, JUDGES, LAWYERS, AND PRISON AUTHORITIES—ARE ONLY TOO CONSCIOUS OF THE HEAVY MORAL BURDEN THEY HAVE ASSUMED. THE prosecutor WHO CALLS ON THE COURT TO IMPOSE THE DEATH PENALTY, THE JUDGES AND JURIES WHOSE DECISION IT IS: ALL THESE ACT IN THE AWARENESS THAT THEIR PLACE IN THE JUDICIAL PROCESS HAS GIVEN THEM EXTRAORDINARY POWERS OVER LIFE AND DEATH.

The prison officials and staff who have the task of carrying out the execution realize that only the gravest of offenses could conceivably justify the taking of another life. Hence, the extensive and elaborate system of safeguards and appeal procedures that allow the course of justice to be halted at any point, if even the slightest doubt should arise that justice is not being done. However, so complicated

Protesters against the death penalty take their message to the streets in Indiana.

a system takes a great deal of time; it may take years to exhaust the possibilities of appeal, throughout which period the prisoner resides on what is popularly referred to as **death row**. This is both a physical location in the jail, set apart from the rest, and a separate psychological place between life and death, another world, with its own customs, its own ways.

In April 2015, 3,002 people were living under the sentence of death in U.S. prisons. Of these, 746 were in California, the United States's largest death row. Next came Florida with 401 convicts and Texas with 271. The racial breakout was the following: 1,284 defendants were white, 1,251 were black, and 386 were Latino. Only 54 of the death row inmates were female.

Life on Death Row

At the beginning of 2002, the state of Colorado had six inmates on death row: all male, their ages ranged from 26 to 46. One prisoner, Frank Rodriguez, had been convicted in 1987 of the rape and murder of a Denver bookkeeper. A decade and a half on death row may sound like a long time, but Rodriguez's case was by no means unusual. Across the United States, the average gap between conviction and execution is around eight years.

Laws unto Themselves

The old Soviet ways seem to be dying hard in Russia and Ukraine, both of which are currently under threat of expulsion from the Council of Europe. Although nominally committed to an impressive-sounding system of checks and balances, evidence has been piling up in recent years that the authorities have been quietly dispensing with jury trials and even carrying out executions in secret, making a mockery of those provisions, which, in theory, exist for appeal.

Though appalled, international observers have hardly been surprised at these revelations. Under both the czarist and Communist regimes, Russia and Ukraine were highly authoritarian, even militaristic, societies. Neither legal system had any tradition of allowing the judgments of ranking officials to be questioned, and execution has always been by firing squad, in the military manner.

Texas prisoner Genaro Camacho Jr. looks out from the semi-darkness of his death row cell. Inmates will typically spend years here before going on to face their final punishment.

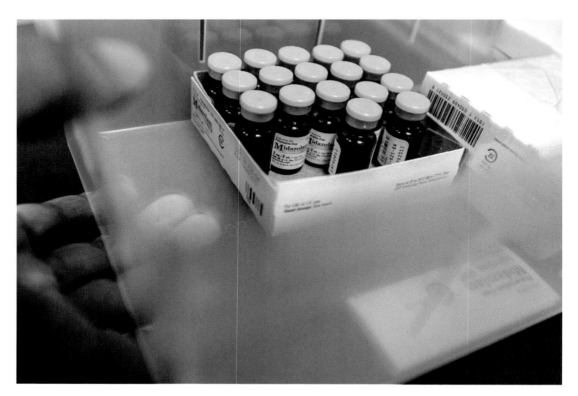

A pharmacist opens a drawer of midazolam, the drug used in executions as a sedative. The U.S. Supreme Court has ruled that its use for execution does not violate the Eighth Amendment ban on cruel and unusual punishment.

In a complicated case, or where (as with Colorado) the state has a tradition of reluctance to execute, longer stays on death row are quite routine. No other Colorado inmate had been there as long as Rodriguez, however. Next in seniority came Robert Harlan (born July 7, 1964), convicted in 1995 of the murder of a casino waitress and the attempted murder of another woman who had come to her aid. The youngest and the oldest inmates, as it happens, had both been convicted as recently as 2000: George Woldt (born November 8, 1976), for the murder of a female college student, and William "Cody" Neal, who carried out the execution-style murder of three women in Jefferson County.

Death row is a separate facility at the Colorado State Penitentiary. Inmates remain there, in single cells, until their appointed "warrant week"—the week of execution—when they are moved to a separate holding cell in the execution suite.

Texas death row inmate Syed Rabbani (above) claims to be a Bangladeshi diplomat being held as a political prisoner.

Only when he has been safely installed in his cell may New Mexico inmate Timothy Allen have his handcuffs removed: for obvious reasons, any movement within the prison has to be conducted with the utmost security.

Death row was designed with security in mind, not beauty or a welcoming atmosphere: here, a guard walks through "A" Pod, "F" section of the Polunsky Unit, Livingston, Texas. Death row security personnel have to be ready for any eventuality from these highly dangerous prisoners.

Death Row

For the sake of security, these dangerous inmates are locked down in their cells for 23 hours a day, with an hour allowed for exercise and showering. If they have to be moved for any reason, it will be with "full restraint" (in cuffs and ankle irons) and under the supervision of at least two prison guards.

For security's sake, all essential services are brought to the inmates in their cells. This includes any medication, educational materials, library books, and food. Visits (two and a half hours a week) with family, lawyers, or media are held in a designated area within the facility, where no physical contact with outsiders can be made. Three times a day—and on extra occasions as necessary—a formal count is held to ensure that all inmates are safely in their cells. The Colorado system allows inmates a TV, radio, newspapers, magazines, and two books at a time in their cells. The days can pass extraordinarily slowly on death row. Access is allowed to the facility's own general and law libraries and to movies shown regularly by the authorities. There are three meals a day. Lower-category prisoners in another part of the penitentiary do cooking, and prison officers bring them across to death row.

A Voice from Death Row

The following is an entry from the journal of David Paul Hammer, awaiting execution at Terre Haute, Indiana, for Wednesday, December 12, 2001.

"After hours of restless sleep where I tossed and turned, I decided to get up. The sun won't be up for hours, and the silence of the Row is creepy. The place has a dead feel to it. The only sounds I've heard were those of the officers doing their count, flashlights beamed into cells of sleeping convicts, nothing appears amiss, so they move on, and then out of hearing range. The only noise to alert me to their presence is the steady jingling of keys as they climb the stairs or walk the tiers. All is quiet now.

"I stood at my cell window, watching nothing but the dead of night. Only a few feet from this unit is the top of the building housing the prison commissary. The roof of that structure is covered with stones the size of golf balls, all shapes and colors. In the pale yellow glow cast by the security light, these rocks seem to glow. Razor-sharp wire in coils are affixed atop the roof's edge to prevent anyone from climbing onto the building...Alone in the early morning hours, my mind screams. There's no escape from the reminders that surround me. Prison...my home."

A wary guard looks on as Arkansas inmate Eugene Wallace Perry is prepared for a visit: outside his cell, the prisoner's every move is carefully controlled. Many death row inmates are highly dangerous people.

Death row inmate Edward Briggs sit in his cell at San Quentin Prison, near Sacramento. Originally built to house fewer than 100 inmates, the prison holds about 600 prisoners.

Warrant Week

When warrant week comes, the routine shifts up a notch, and extra visiting privileges are routinely granted at this time. On the day of the execution, after meeting with an approved spiritual adviser in preparation for death, the inmate will have his traditional choice of "last meal" at the normal time. He may choose anything the

Daniel Gardner, son of convicted killer Ronnie Lee Gardner wipes tears from his eyes just before the execution of his father by firing squad outside the Utah State Prison. The killer decided to die by rifle fire over lethal injection, a choice he was given because he was convicted before 2004, when Utah did away with firing squad executions.

prison's food service department has in stock at the time. Ninety minutes before execution, he is allowed to shower and change into a clean green uniform: pants, button-up shirt, socks, and shoes. Thirty minutes before the appointed time, he is taken from his cell by a specialized "strap down" team, who will ensure that he is properly fastened down on the execution bed. With around 20 minutes still to run, the IV team will insert the drips for the lethal injection: ample time must be allowed for what can, on occasion, be a tricky procedure.

After the warden has read the execution warrant to the prisoner–usually with around eight minutes still remaining–selected witnesses will be ushered into an adjacent observation room. These will generally include close family members, the prosecuting and defense attorneys, and a member of the law enforcement agency who first brought the prisoner to justice, in addition to approved representatives of the media.

Up until this point, the execution chamber can be contacted by telephone, just in case a reprieve or stay of execution should come through. Now, however, it is deemed that the proceedings have reached the point of no return, and the warden formally disconnects the telephone. The order is then given for the lethal injection to be administered. Two minutes later, the coroner is asked to enter the chamber to pronounce death and record the time. Once this has been done, the witnesses are escorted to the lobby of the execution suite to sign the record of execution.

Escaping the Finality

The death penalty is society's ultimate sanction, and it is never imposed lightly. An elaborate system of checks and balances exists to prevent the possibility of error or injustice. There are two separate systems of appeals, state and federal. In fact, the former arguably constitutes two systems in itself, since the prisoner can first appeal the sentence directly all the way up to the United States Supreme Court, then if that fails, start all over again, appealing particular technical details of his trial to ever-higher levels.

If sympathetic to the arguments made on a prisoner's behalf, the state governor may intervene in the process, in some cases ordering a "commutation of sentence" (a reduction from death penalty to life imprisonment) or even a complete **pardon**. More often, he or she will issue a temporary reprieve or stay of execution to allow a particular point of law or investigative angle to be explored.

For many prisoners, the research and work involved in pursuing the possible legal avenues can become an occupation, offering a sense of purpose in life (and, in some cases, the start of an academic interest). For society at large, all these

Bill Pelke at the grave of his grandmother, Ruth Pelke a 78-year-old Gary, Indiana Bible teacher. Ruth was murdered in May 1985. Paula Cooper was convicted and sentenced to death for the crime, but later had her sentence commuted to life in prison. Pelke became an opponent of the death penalty.

procedures are a mixed blessing. At best, they introduce bureaucratic complexity and lengthy delays to the administration of the death penalty. At worst, they open the system up to cynical exploitation, although this is generally regarded as a price worth paying. Better the abuse of such safeguards by the guilty than that an unwarranted execution should take place and a man or woman be killed unjustly.

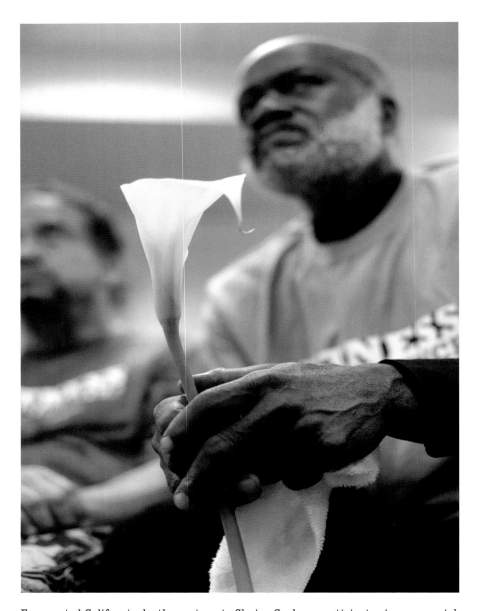

Exonerated California death row inmate Shujaa Graham participates in a memorial service for an executed Georgia inmate during the Witness to Innocence summit in Norcross, Georgia. The meeting, which included 25 exonerated death row inmates, was held to fight against the prevalence of the death penalty in the southern United States.

And there are precedents for the system getting it wrong. Research suggests that the rate of wrongful convictions for murder and sexual assault runs between 3 percent and 5 percent.

Text-Dependent Questions

1. What is the racial breakdown of prisoners on death row?
2. What is a "warrant week"?
3. How can prisoners on death row entertain themselves?
4. What is a pardon?

Research Projects

1. Choose an inmate currently or formerly on death row. Find out what he did to get there: what crimes did he commit? What arguments did the defense attorney present at trial? What sort of testimony did the prosecutor bring against him? Then investigate his experience on death row. What prison was he in? What were conditions like there? How long has he been there, or how long was he there before he was executed or released? Has he submitted appeals claiming innocence? If he has not yet been executed, what method is the state likely to use? If he has been executed, how was it done? Did it go smoothly?

2. Investigate DNA sequencing. How is it done? How reliable is it? Do you think DNA evidence as used is a good basis for sentencing someone to death?

3. Go to the website of the Innocence Project. Choose an inmate whose case the project is currently investigating. Research the case against him. Decide whether you think there is sufficient certainty about his crime to sentence him to death.

SERIES GLOSSARY

Amnesty: pardon given by a country to citizens who have committed crimes

Anarchist: a person who wants to do away with organized society and government

Antiglobalization: against large companies or economies spreading into other nations

Appeal: referral of a case to a higher court for review

Arraignment: a formal court hearing at which the prisoner is asked whether he or she pleads "guilty" or "not guilty" to the charge or charges

Bifurcated: divided into two branches or parts

Bioassay: chemical analysis of biological samples

Biometrics: use of physical characteristics, such as fingerprints and voice, to identify users

Certificate of certiorari: a document that a losing party files with the Supreme Court, asking the Supreme Court to review the decision of a lower court it includes a list of the parties, a statement of the facts of the case, and arguments as to why the court should grant the writ

Circumstantial evidence: evidence that can contribute to the conviction of an accused person but that is not considered sufficient without eyewitness or forensic evidence

Civil disobedience: refusing, in a peaceful way, to obey a government policy or law

Clemency: an act of leniency or mercy, especially to moderate the severity of punishment due

Commute: to change a penalty to another one less severe

Cryptology: the science and art of making and breaking codes and ciphers

Dactylography: the original name for the taking and analysis of fingerprints

Deputy: a person appointed as a substitute with power to act

Dissident: someone who disagrees with an established religious or political system, organization, or belief

Distributed Denial of Service (DDOS) attack: a malware attack that floods all the bandwidth of a system or server, causing the system to be unable to service real business

Effigy: a model or dummy of someone

Electronic tagging: the attaching of an electronic device to a criminal after he or she has been released, in order to track the person to ensure that he or she does not commit a crime again

Ethics: the discipline dealing with what is good and bad and with moral duty and obligation

Euthanasia: the act of killing or permitting the death of hopelessly sick or injured individuals in a relatively painless way for reasons of mercy

Exhume: to dig up a corpse, usually for examination

Exoneration: a finding that a person is not in fact guilty of the crime for which he or she has been accused

Extortion: the act of obtaining money from a person by force, intimidation, or undue or illegal power

Forensics: the scientific analysis and review of the physical and medical evidence of a crime

Garrote: to strangle someone using a thin wire with handles at either end

Gibbet: an upright post with a projecting arm for hanging the bodies of executed criminals as a warning

Graft: the acquisition of gain (as money) in dishonest or questionable ways

Grievance: a real or imagined wrong, for which there are thought to be reasonable grounds for complaint

Heresy: religious convictions contrary to church dogma and that deviate from orthodox belief

Hulk: a ship used as a prison

Hypostasis: the migration of blood to the lowest parts of a dead body, caused by the effect of gravity

Incendiary: a bomb

Infiltrate: to enter or become established in gradually or unobtrusively, usually for subversive purposes

Intern (v.): to confine or impound, especially during a war

Interpol: an association of national police forces that promotes cooperation and mutual assistance in apprehending international criminals and criminals who flee abroad to avoid justice

Intrusion detection system (IDS): software designed to detect misuse of a system

Junta: a group of military officers who hold power, usually as the result of a coup

Jurisprudence: a system or body of law

Ladder: an early form of the rack in which the victim was tied to a vertical framework and weights were attached to his ankles

Lag: a convict

Latent: present and capable of becoming obvious, or active, even though not currently visible

Lockstep: a mode of marching in step where people move one after another as closely as possible

Lynch: to attack and kill a person, typically by hanging, without involvement of the courts or legal system and often done by a mob

Manifesto: a written statement declaring publicly the intentions, motives, or views of its issuer

Manslaughter: the unlawful killing of a human being without express or implied intent

Martyrdom: the suffering of death on account of adherence to a cause and especially to one's religious faith

Mercenary: a man or woman who is paid by a foreign government or organization to fight in its service

Miscreant: one who behaves criminally or viciously

Molotov cocktail: an explosive weapon; each "cocktail" is a bottle filled with gasoline and wrapped in a rag or plugged with a wick, then ignited and thrown

Money laundering: to transfer illegally obtained money through an outside party to conceal the true source

Mule: a person who smuggles drugs inside his or her body

Mutinous: to resist lawful authority

Paramilitary: of, relating to, being, or characteristic of a force formed on a military pattern, especially as a potential auxiliary military force

Pathologist: a physician who specializes in examining tissue samples and fluids to diagnose diseases

PCR: polymerase chain reaction, a technique of making multiple copies of a small section of DNA so that it can be analyzed and identified

Personal alarm: a small electronic device that a person can carry and activate if he or she feels threatened

Phreaker: a person who hacks telephone systems

Pillory: a device formerly used for publicly punishing offenders consisting of a wooden frame with holes in which the head and hands can be locked

Political asylum: permitting foreigners to settle in your country to escape danger in another country, usually his or her native land

Postmortem: an autopsy; an examination of a dead body, looking for causes of death

Precedent: something done or said that serves as an example or rule to authorize or justify a subsequent act of similar kind

Pyramid scheme: an investment swindle in which some early investors are paid off with money put up by later ones in order to encourage more and bigger risks; also called a Ponzi scheme

Quick: the living flesh beneath the fingernails

Racketeering: the act of conducting a fraudulent scheme or activity

Ratchet: a mechanism consisting of a "pawl," a hinged catch that slips into sloping teeth of a cogwheel, so that it can be turned only in one direction

Repatriation: returning a person to his or her country of origin

Ruse: a subterfuge in order to distract someone's attention

Screw: slang term for a prison guard

Scuttle: to cut a hole through the bottom, deck, or side of a ship

Seditious: of, relating to, or tending toward an incitement of resistance to or insurrection against lawful authority

Serology: the laboratory analysis of blood serum, particularly in the detection of blood groups and antibodies

Siege (n.): a standoff situation, in which a group holds a position by force and refuses to surrender

Slander: a false and defamatory oral statement about a person

Smash and grab: a term used to describe a method of stealing, where thieves break windows (for example, on a shop front or a car) to grab the goods within before fleeing

Statute: a law enacted by the legislative branch of a government

Statutory: authorized by the statute that defines the law

Subversive: characterized by systematic attempts to overthrow or undermine a government or political system by persons working secretly from within

Succinylcholine: a synthetic drug that paralyzes muscle fiber

Vendetta: an often-prolonged series of retaliatory, vengeful, or hostile acts or exchange of such acts

White-collar crime: crime committed by office staff, usually involving theft from the company they work for

Worm: a computer program that enters one computer and replicates itself to spread to other computers; unlike a virus, it does not have to attach itself to other files

Xenophobic: having an unreasonable fear of what is foreign and especially of people of foreign origin

CHRONOLOGY

1775 B.C.: Babylonian Code of Hammurabi, the first known legal system.

800: Early Romans throw traitors to their deaths from the Tarpeian Rock.

100: Their empire expanding into the Middle East, the Romans are influenced by local practices, such as crucifixion.

A.D. 1608: Captain George Kendall is executed; this is the first recorded case in the American colonies.

1632: Jane Champion is executed; she is the first woman known to have been executed in the American colonies.

1744: Empress Elizabeth abolishes the death penalty in Russia.

1764: Cesare Bonesana Beccaria's *Essay on Crimes and Punishments* is published; it was considered the classic expression of Enlightenment thinking on this issue.

1834: Pennsylvania moves executions inside correctional facilities.

1845: The American Society for the Abolition of Capital Punishment is established.

1859: John Brown is executed in Charles Town, in what is now West Virginia.

1892: Newton Curtis introduces his (unsuccessful) bill for complete abolition of capital punishment at a federal level.

1897: "An Act to Reduce the Cases in Which the Death Penalty May be Inflicted" is passed by Congress.

1846: Michigan abolishes the death penalty for all crimes except treason.

1890: William Kemmler is the first person to die in the electric chair.

1924: Nevada becomes the first state to use cyanide gas in executions; the refusal of a Chicago court to give the death sentence in the case of "Thrill Killers" Richard Loeb and Nathan Leopold Jr. causes public outcry.

1927: The execution of Nicola Sacco and Bartolomeo Vanzetti causes another public outcry.

1958: *Trop v. Dulles* Supreme Court judgment acknowledges the possibility that standards of decency may change in a "maturing society."

1965: Hanging is abolished in Britain.

1972: *Furman v. Georgia* judgment effectively abolishes the death penalty in the United States.

1976: *Gregg v. Georgia* effectively reinstates the death penalty.

1977: Gary Gilmore is executed by a Utah firing squad; Oklahoma becomes the first state to use lethal injection in executions.

1996: European Union makes complete abolition of capital punishment a condition of membership; for most member states, this means little more than the formal confirmation of existing laws.

2001: Oklahoma City bomber Timothy McVeigh executed by lethal injection in Indiana.

2015: U.S. Supreme Court upholds use of the sedative midazolam in executions in *Glossip v. Gross*.

FURTHER INFORMATION

Useful Web Sites

Death Penalty Information Center: www.deathpenaltyinfo.org

Amnesty International: www.amnestyinternational.org

The Innocence Project: www.innocenceproject.org

Death Penalty ProCon: deathpenalty.procon.org

How Lethal Injection Works: people.howstuffworks.com/lethal-injection.htm

Further Reading

Banner, Stuart. *The Death Penalty: An American History*. Cambridge, MA: Harvard University Press, 2002.

Garfield, David. *The Death Penalty: Capital Punishment in the USA*. Amazon Digital Services, 2015.

Lyon, Andrea. *The Death Penalty: What's Keeping It Alive*. Rowman & Littlefield, 2014.

Sarat, Austin. *Gruesome Spectacles: Botched Executions and America's Death Penalty*. Stanford, CA: Stanford Law Books, 2014.

Solotaroff, Ivan. *The Last Face You'll Ever See: The Private Life of the American Death Penalty*. New York: HarperCollins, 2001.

About the Author

Michael Kerrigan was born in Liverpool, England, and educated at St. Edward's College, from where he won an Open Scholarship to University College, Oxford. He lived for a time in the United States, spending time first at Princeton, followed by a period working in publishing in New York. Since then he has been a free-lance writer and journalist, with commissions across a wide range of subjects, but with a special interest in social policy and defense issues. Within this field, he has written on every region of the world.

His work has been published by leading international educational publishers, including the BBC, Dorling Kindersley, Time-Life, and Reader's Digest Books. His work as a journalist includes regular contributions to the *Times Literary Supplement*, London, as well as a weekly column in the *Scotsman* newspaper, Edinburgh, where he now lives with his wife and their two children.

INDEX

PICTURE CREDITS

Front Cover: Subsociety/iStock

Picture Credits: 8, Mary Evans Picture Library; 11, Mary Evans Picture Library; 12, Mary Evans Picture Library; 13, Mary Evans Picture Library; 14, Mary Evans Picture Library; 17, Mary Evans Picture Library; 18, AKG London; 18, Mary Evans Picture Library; 19, AKG London; 20, Popperfoto; 22, Mary Evans Picture Library; 24, Popperfoto; 27, Mary Evans Picture Library; 29, Mary Evans Picture Library; 30, Mary Evans Picture Library; 31, Mary Evans Picture Library; 33, AKG London; 34, Topham Picturepoint; 36, Topham Picturepoint; 37, Topham Picturepoint; 38, Popperfoto; 39, Topham Picturepoint; 40, Popperfoto; 42, Topham Picturepoint; 45, Amber Books; 46, Popperfoto; 47, Topham Picturepoint; 48, Popperfoto; 48, Topham Picturepoint; 50, Topham Picturepoint; 51, Topham Picturepoint; 53, EyeJoy/iStock; 54, Topham Picturepoint; 56, Mary Evans Picture Library; 58, Fbi/Zuma Press/Newscom; 59, Topham Picturepoint; 60, Topham Picturepoint; 62, Topham Picturepoint; 63, Topham Picturepoint; 65, Popperfoto; 66, Topham Picturepoint; 67, Tina Norris/REX/Newscom and Kyodo/Newscom; 68, Janet Meyer/Splash News/Newscom; 70, Jeffrey Phelps/KRT/Newscom; 73, Topham Picturepoint; 74, Stuart Isett/Polaris/Newscom; 75, Topham Picturepoint; 76, Topham Picturepoint; 77, Popperfoto; 79, Topham Picturepoint; 80, Brian Baer/Zuma Press/Newscom; 81, George Frey/EPA/Newscom; 83, Susan Plageman/KRT/Newscom; 84, Erik S. Lesser/EPA/Newscom